THE BIBLE OF FRITTERS AND FRENCH FRIES

A Fried Cookbook with Over 100 Delicious Fritter Recipes and French Fry Recipes

Nora Rose

All rights reserved.
Disclaimer

The information contained i is meant to serve as a comprehensive collection of strategies that the author of this eBook has done research about. Summaries, strategies, tips and tricks are only recommendation by the author, and reading this eBook will not guarantee that one's results will exactly mirror the author's results. The author of the eBook has made all reasonable effort to provide current and accurate information for the readers of the eBook. The author and it's associates will not be held liable for any unintentional error or omissions that may be found. The material in the eBook may include information by third parties. Third party materials comprise of opinions expressed by their owners. As such, the author of the eBook does not assume responsibility or liability for any third party material or opinions. Whether because of the progression of the internet, or the unforeseen changes in company policy and editorial submission guidelines, what is stated as fact at the time of this writing may become outdated or inapplicable later.

The eBook is copyright © 2021 with all rights reserved. It is illegal to redistribute, copy, or create derivative work from this eBook whole or in part. No parts of this report may be reproduced or retransmitted in any reproduced or retransmitted in any forms whatsoever without the writing expressed and signed permission from the author.

INTRODUCTION	9
CEREAL, NUTS & SEEDS FRITTERS	11
1. Quick brown rice fritters	11
2. Corn fritters	13
3. Black eyed pea fritters	15
4. Rice fritters	17
5. Blueberry/corn fritters	19
6. Corn fritters with dipping sauce	21
7. Carnival fritters	23
8. Garbanzo fritters with pear salsa	25
9. Chickpea fritters with couscous	27
10. Corn & pepper fritters	29
11. Chanuka fritters	31
VEGETABLE FRITTERS	33
12. Okra fritters	33
13. Bean fritters	35
14. Gingered sweet-potato fritters	37
15. Aubergine fritters	39
16. Artichoke fritters	41
17. Rhubarb chard fritters	43
18. Fig fritters	45
19. Mixed-greens with turnip fritters	47
20. Dessert zucchini fritters	49
21. Leek fritters	51
22. Lentil fritters and beet Vinaigrette	53

23.	Eggplant fritter	55
24.	Curried carrot fritters	57
25.	Fried pea fritters	59
26.	Stuffed potato fritters	61
27.	Mushroom fritters	63
28.	Onion bhajiyas / onion fritters	65
29.	Pakora	67
30.	Parsnip and carrot fritters	69
31.	Pomme frites/patatine fritters	71
32.	Potato and walnut fritters	73
33.	Pumpkin fritters	75
34.	Spinach fritters	77
35.	Deep fried tofu fritters	79
36.	Tomato fritters	81

FRUIT FRITTERS 83

37.	Dutch apple fritters	83
38.	Apple-orange fritters	85
39.	Banana fritters in tempura batter	87
40.	Apricot fritters	89
41.	Benya banana fritters	91
42.	Langoustine and banana fritter	93
43.	Canned peach fritters	95
44.	Caribbean pineapple fritters	97
45.	Elderberry fritters	99
46.	Fruit and vegetable fritters	101
47.	Fruit fritters with lemon-bourbon sauce	103

48.	Northern spy apple fritters	105
49.	Pineapple banana fritters	107
50.	Poached pear fritters	110
51.	Catfish fritters	112
52.	Codfish fritters	114
53.	Fish and crab meat fritters	116
54.	cape cod clam & corn fritters	118
55.	Conch fritters	120
56.	Canned clam fritters	122
57.	Crab & avocado fritters	124
58.	Crawfish fritters	126
59.	Clam fritters	128
60.	Indonesian corn shrimp fritters	130
61.	Italian spaghetti squash fritters	132
62.	Lobster fritters	134
63.	Mussel fritters with salsa	136
64.	Octopus fritters	138
65.	Shrimp fritter	140
66.	Oyster corn fritters	142
67.	Tuna fritters	144
CHEESE FRITTERS		**146**
68.	Basle cheese fritters	146
69.	Herb fritters with yoghurt apricot dip	148
70.	Bern cheese fritters	150
71.	Bean, corn & cheddar fritters	152
72.	Mozzarella fritters and spaghetti	154

73.	Emmenthal cheese fritters	156
74.	Cornmeal cheddar fritters	158
75.	Camembert fritters	160
76.	Cauliflower-cheddar fritters	162
77.	Cheese stuffed potato fritters	164
78.	Pear and cheddar fritters	166
79.	Ricotta and chestnut fritters with bagna cauda	168
80.	Waadtland cheese fritters	170

MEATS & POULTRY FRITTERS 172

81.	Chicken fritters	172
82.	Chunky beef fritters	174
83.	Egg fritters with string beans and macaroni	176
84.	Fresh corn & sausage fritters	178
85.	Hot dog corn fritters	180
86.	Korean meat fritters	182
87.	Parmesan and mozzarella fritters	184

DESSERT FRITTERS 186

88.	Chocolate-covered pecan fritters	186
89.	Choux fritters	188
90.	Christmas pudding fritters	190
91.	Cinnamon fritters	192
92.	French fritters	194
93.	Maple fritters	196
94.	Rum cherry fritters	198
95.	Suvganiot	200
96.	Wine fritters	202

EDIBLE FLOWER FRITTTERS 204
   97. Elderflower fritters served with elderflower mousse 204
   98. Dandelion flower fritters 206
   99. Elderflower fritters 208
   100. Rose petal fritters.. 210

CONCLUSION 212

INTRODUCTION

By definition, fritters are basically fried food categorised broadly into three categories:

- Deep-fried cakes of Chou paste or a yeast dough.
- Bits of meat, seafood, vegetables, or fruit coated with a batter and deep fried.
- Small cakes of chopped food in batter, such as corn fritters.

Fritters are an extremely versatile food. They can be a side dish, appetizer, snack, or dessert. They were originally introduced in Japan in the 16th century, and have been increasingly popular in this decade.

Basic Tips to get started

1. Don't be scared of oil. Make sure you add enough to the pan, as it will help to give crispiness, good colour and delicious flavour to the fritters.

2. Let it sizzle! Your pan needs to be properly heated up before cooking. If the fritter doesn't sizzle when it hits the pan, you know it's not ready!

3. Don't overcrowd the pan, as this causes the temperature of the pan to drop, resulting in limp, under-cooked fritters.

The Basic Formula

Veggies + Aromatics & Spices + Cheese + Binding Agent

CEREAL, NUTS & SEEDS FRITTERS

1. Quick brown rice fritters

Yield: 6 Serving

Ingredient

- 2 cups Cooked short grain brown rice
- ½ cup Sugar
- 3 Eggs; beaten
- ½ teaspoon Salt
- ¼ teaspoon Vanilla
- 6 tablespoons Flour

- ½ teaspoon Nutmeg
- 3 teaspoons Baking powder

Combine rice, eggs, vanilla, and nutmeg and mix well.

Sift dry ingredients together and stir into rice mixture. Drop by spoonfuls into hot deep fat (360) and fry until brown.

Drain on absorbent paper, sprinkle with powdered sugar and serve hot

2. Corn fritters

Yield: 4 Serving

Ingredient

- 10 ounces Green giant frozen cream style

- corn Oil for deep frying
- ½ cup Flour
- ½ cup Yellow cornmeal
- 1 teaspoon Baking powder
- 1 teaspoon Instant minced onion
- ½ teaspoon Salt
- 2 Eggs

Place unopened corn pouch in warm water for 10 to 15 minutes to thaw.

In deep fat fryer or heavy saucepan, heat 2 to 3 inches of oil to 375 degrees. In medium bowl, combine thawed corn and remaining ingredients; stir until well combined.

Drop batter by level tablespoonful's into hot oil, 375 degrees. Fry 2 to 3 minutes or until golden brown. Drain on paper towel

3. Black eyed pea fritters

Yield: 20 Serving

Ingredient

- ½ pounds Black-eyed peas, soaked
- 4 each Garlic cloves, crushed
- 2 teaspoons Salt
- 1 teaspoon Black pepper
- 4 tablespoons Water
- Oil for frying

- Lime juice to taste

When peas have softened, rub off skins, and soak an additional 30 minutes.

Drain & rinse.

In a food processor, process peas, garlic, salt & pepper

Add water while continuing to process. Add enough water to get a smooth, thick purée.

Preheat oven to 250F. In a large skillet, heat 2 to 3 inches oil & fry 1 tub of the batter till its golden brown. Repeat till all the batter has been fried in this way. Keep in oven to keep hot. Serve piping hot, sprinkled with salt & lime juice.

4. Rice fritters

Yield: 12 Serving

Ingredient

- 1 pack Dry yeast
- 2 tablespoons Warm water
- 1½ cup Cooked rice; cooled
- 3 Eggs; beaten
- 1½ cup Flour
- ½ cup Sugar

- ½ teaspoon Salt
- ¼ teaspoon Nutmeg
- Fat for deep frying
- Confectioner's sugar

Dissolve yeast in warm water. Mix with rice and let stand in a warm spot overnight. The following day, beat in eggs, flour, sugar, salt and nutmeg.

Add more flour if necessary to make a thick batter. Heat fat to 370 degrees or until a 1-inch bread cube browns in 60 seconds. Drop batter from a tablespoon into hot grease and fry until golden brown, about 3 minutes.

Drain on paper towels and sprinkle with powdered sugar. Serve hot

5. Blueberry/corn fritters

Yield: 6 Serving

Ingredient

- ⅔ cup Flour
- ⅓ cup Cornstarch
- 2 tablespoons Sugar
- 1 teaspoon Baking powder
- ½ teaspoon Salt
- ¼ tablespoon Nutmeg, ground
- ⅓ cup Milk

- 2 Egg, separated
- Vegetable oil
- 1½ cup Blueberries
- Confectioner's sugar & Honey

In medium bowl, stir together flour, cornstarch, sugar, baking powder, salt, and nutmeg.

In 2 cup measuring cup, stir together milk, egg yolks, and oil. Pour into flour mixture. Mix well. Batter will be stiff. Stir in blueberries. Set aside.

In small bowl with mixer on high, beat egg whites until stiff peaks form. With rubber spatula, gently fold half of beaten egg whites into batter until well blended. Then fold remaining beaten egg whites into batter,

Carefully add fritter batter by tablespoonful's, a few at a time, to hot oil. Fry 3-4 minutes, turning once, or until fritters are golden brown.

6. Corn fritters with dipping sauce

Yield: 8 Serving

Ingredient

- 2 large Eggs; beaten
- ¾ cup Milk
- 1 teaspoon Ground cumin
- 2 cups Flour
- Salt and pepper to taste
- 2 cups Corn Kernels
- 3 tablespoons Parsley; chopped

Spicy Orange Sauce

- ½ cup Orange marmalade
- 1⅜ cup Fresh orange juice
- 1 tablespoon Ginger; grated
- ½ teaspoon Dijon-style mustard

In bowl, beat eggs and milk. In another bowl, stir the cumin over the flour. Season well with salt and pepper

Beat the egg mixture into the flour with a whisk. Stir in corn and parsley. Heat oil to 375° Drop the corn mixture into the hot fat without crowding the pan. Fry, turning once, until golden brown

Remove and drain on paper towels. Combine Sauce ingredients & serve.

7. Carnival fritters

Yield: 18 Serving

Ingredient

- 1 cup Hot Water
- 8 tablespoons Unsalted Butter
- 1 tablespoon Sugar
- ½ teaspoon Salt
- 1 cup All-Purpose Flour, Sifted
- 4 Eggs
- 1 teaspoon Freshly Grated Orange Rind

-
-

    1 teaspoon Freshly Grated Lemon Rind

    4 cups Peanut Oil·

- Confectioners' Sugar

Combine the water, butter, sugar, and salt in a small sauce pan and bring to a boil. When butter is melted, add flour. Stir vigorously with a whisk

Add the eggs, one at a time, beating vigorously with a spoon after each addition. Add the grated orange and lemon rinds.

In a deep skillet, heat the peanut oil to 300° F.

Drop the batter by the tablespoonful into the hot oil, no more than 4 or 5 at a time. When the fritters are browned and puffed, remove them with a slotted spoon, drain on paper towels, and sprinkle with confectioners' sugar.

8. Garbanzo fritters with pear salsa

Yield: 1 Serving

Ingredient

- 1½ cup Cooked garbanzos, drained
- 1 teaspoon Salt
- 1 medium Idaho potato
- 1 small Onion, coarsely grated
- 1 tablespoon Flour
-
-

-
-

  2 teaspoons Hot pepper sauce

  3 Egg whites, lightly beaten

  2 Italian plum tomatoes

  2 Firm pears peeled, cored, and diced

- 1 tablespoon Fresh lemon juice
- 6 large Scallions, chopped
- 1 tablespoon Jalapeño peppers
- 1 tablespoon Sherry wine vinegar
- 1 teaspoon Honey

In a medium bowl, combine the potato, onion, flour, and hot pepper sauce. Mix well to blend. Add garbanzo beans and egg whites and mix.

Drop rounded tablespoons of the batter into the skillet allowing room for them to spread. Cook over moderately high heat until they are golden brown

Serve with Zesty Pear Salsa

9. Chickpea fritters with couscous

Yield: 1 Serving

Ingredient

- 7 ounces Couscous,cooked
- ½ small Cucumber
- 2 Plum tomatoes; (peeled, seeded, diced)
- 1 Lime
- 6 Green onions; trimmed
-
-

-
-
    1 can (14oz) chickpeas drained rinsed

    ½ teaspoon Coriander or cilantro and mint

    1 Red chili; seeded finely chopped

    1 Garlic clove

- Plain flour for dusting
- 5 ounces FF yoghurt
- Salt & freshly ground pepper
- Paprika/Cumin to taste

Stir tomatoes, parsley into couscous. Halve lime and squeeze in the juice. Finely chop spring onions into couscous.

Add cumin, coriander/cilantro, chili and coriander/cilantro leaves. Chop garlic clove and add. Place cucumber in a bowl and stir in yoghurt chop mint add with plenty of seasoning. Mix well

Shape chickpea mixture into 6 patties and dust lightly with flour. Add to the pan and cook for a few minutes.

10. Corn & pepper fritters

Yield: 12 Fritters

Ingredient

- 1¼ cup Corn, whole-kernel, fresh or frozen
- 1 cup Bell pepper, red; finely chopped
- 1 cup Scallions; finely chopped
- 1 teaspoon Jalapeño; finely minced
- 1 teaspoon Ground cumin
-
-

-
-
    - 1¼ cup Flour
    - 2 teaspoons Baking powder
    - Salt; to taste
    - Pepper, black; to taste
- 1 cup Milk
- 4 tablespoons Oil

Put the corn in a mixing bowl along with the chopped pepper, scallions, and hot pepper. Sprinkle with the cumin, flour, baking powder, salt, and pepper; stir to blend. Add the milk and stir to blend thoroughly.

Spoon the batter in ¼ cup batches into the skillet and cook until golden brown on both sides, about 2 minutes each.

11. Chanuka fritters

Yield: 1 Serving

Ingredient

- 2 Yeast, active dry envelopes Warm water
- 2½ cup Flour; unbleached up to 3 Salt
- 2 teaspoons Anise seeds
- 2 tablespoons Olive oil
- 1 cup Raisins; seedless dark
- 1 cup Olive oil for frying
- 1½ cup Honey

- 2 tablespoons Lemon juice

Combine flour, salt and anise seeds in a bowl. Gradually add the dissolved yeast and the 2 Tbsp olive oil. Knead until dough is smooth and elastic

Spread the raisins over the working surface and knead the dough over them. Shape into a ball.

Heat the oil and fry the diamonds a few at a time, turning, until golden brown on both sides.

Heat the honey in a saucepan with 2 Tbsp of lemon juice and boil for just 3 minutes. Arrange on a serving plate and pour the hot honey over them.

VEGETABLE FRITTERS

12. Okra fritters

Yield: 1 Serving

Ingredient

- 1 cup Sifted unbleached flour
- 1½ teaspoon Baking powder
- 2 teaspoons Salt
- ¼ teaspoon Ground black pepper
- ¼ teaspoon Grated nutmeg

- 1 pinch Cayenne

- 2 cups fresh okra -- thinly sliced

Combine ingredients well

Drop by teaspoons into oil. Cook until golden, 3-5 minutes until they float up, and then turn over.

Drain on paper towels & Serve hot with dipping sauce if desired.

13. Bean fritters

Yield: 24 Fritters

Ingredient

- 1 cup Peas, black-eyed
- 2 Pepper, red, hot; seeded, chopped
- 2 teaspoons Salt
- Oil, vegetable; for frying

Soak the beans overnight in cold water. Drain, rub off and discard the skin, cover beans again with cold water and soak for 2-3 hours longer. Drain, rinse, and put through a meat grinder using the finest blade, or reduce bit by bit in an electric blender. Grind the peppers. Add the salt and peppers to the beans and beat with a wooden spoon until they are light and fluffy and considerably increased in bulk.

Heat the oil in a heavy frying pan and fry the mixture by tablespoonful's until golden brown on both sides. Drain on paper towels. Serve hot as an accompaniment to drinks.

14. Gingered sweet-potato fritters

Yield: 1 Serving

Ingredient

- A; (1/2-pound) sweet potato
- 1½ teaspoon Minced peeled fresh gingerroot
- 2 teaspoons Fresh lemon juice
- ¼ teaspoon Dried hot red pepper flakes
- ¼ teaspoon Salt
- 1 large Egg
- 5 tablespoons All-purpose flour
- Vegetable oil for deep-frying

In a food processor chop fine the grated sweet potato with the gingerroot, the lemon juice, the red pepper flakes, and the salt, add the egg and the flour, and blend the mixture well.

In a large saucepan heat $1\frac{1}{2}$ inches of the oil and drop tablespoons of the sweet-potato mixture into the oil until they are golden

Transfer the fritters to paper towels to drain.

15. Aubergine fritters

Yield: 6 Serving

Ingredient

- 2 Eggs, beaten
- Salt to taste
- 2 tablespoons Milk
- 2 Aubergines (eggplants), finely sliced
- Oil for deep frying

Mix the eggs, salt and milk together to make a batter. Dip the Aubergine slices into the batter and deep-fry the coated Aubergine slices in the oil over moderate heat until evenly brown.

16. Artichoke fritters

Yield: 6 Serving

Ingredient

- ½ pounds Artichoke hearts, cooked and diced
- 4 Eggs, separated
- 1 teaspoon Baking powder
- 3 Green onions, chopped
- 1 tablespoon Grated lemon peel
- ½ cup Flour

- Salt and pepper to taste
- 1 tablespoon Cornstarch
- 4 cups Oil for frying, Peanut or corn oil

Place artichoke hearts in a large bowl and stir in egg yolks and baking powder. Add green onion. Fold in lemon peel. Mix in flour, salt and pepper. In a separate bowl, beat egg whites and cornstarch together until peaks form. Fold egg whites into artichoke mixture.

With a tablespoon, drop half dollar sized dollops of fritter batter into oil. Fry until golden brown

Remove fritters with a slotted spoon and drain on paper towels.

17. Rhubarb chard fritters

Yield: 1 Serving

Ingredient

- 8 Stalks rhubarb chard
- 1 cup Flour
- ½ teaspoon Salt
- ⅛ teaspoon Paprika
- 1 Egg, slightly beaten
- 2 tablespoons Oil or melted butter
- ⅔ cup Milk

- Oil for deep frying

Mix flour, salt, paprika, egg, oil or butter, and milk.

Dip pieces of stem in this batter, covering them well. Fry in deep fat heated to 375 F or until hot enough to brown a 1-inch cube of bread in 1 minute.

Drain on brown paper in a warm oven

18. Fig fritters

Yield: 24 Figs

Ingredient

- 24 Firm ripe figs
- 2 Eggs, separated
- $\frac{5}{8}$ cup Milk
- 1 tablespoon Oil
- 1 pinch Salt
- Grated lemon rind
- $20\frac{1}{2}$ ounce Flour

-
-

1 tablespoon Sugar

Oil for frying

In a bowl beat the egg yolks with the milk, oil, salt and lemon rind. Stir in the flour and sugar and combine well. Refrigerate the batter for 2 hours.

Beat the egg whites until stiff and fold them into the batter. Dip the figs into the batter and fry them in deep, hot oil until golden brown.

Drain briefly and sprinkle with sugar. Apricots, bananas and other fruit can be prepared in the same way.

19. Mixed-greens with turnip fritters

Yield: 6 Serving

Ingredient

- ¼ cup butter
- 1 cup Chopped onion
- 1 cup Chopped green onions
- 2 Stalks celery, chopped
- 2 tablespoons Finely chopped gingerroot
-
-
-

-
-
    - 2 Cloves garlic, finely chopped
    - 1 pounds Baby turnips with green tops
    - 10 cups Water
    - 2 Extra-large chicken bouillon cubes
    - $\frac{1}{2}$ cup Dry white wine or water
- $\frac{1}{4}$ cup Cornstarch
- 6 cups packed whole fresh spinach leaves
- $1\frac{1}{4}$ teaspoon Ground black pepper
- $\frac{1}{2}$ teaspoon Salt
- $\frac{1}{4}$ cup Unsifted all-purpose flour
- 1 Large egg, lightly beaten
- Vegetable oil for frying

Prepare the greens.

Coarsely grate cooled turnips. Combine grated turnips, the flour, egg, and remaining $\frac{1}{4}$ t each of pepper and salt.

Add heaping teaspoonfuls of fritter mixture to skillet and fry, turning, until brown on both sides

20. Dessert zucchini fritters

Yield: 2 Serving

Ingredient

- 2 Eggs
- ⅔ cup Low-fat cottage cheese
- 2 slices White or WW bread crumbled
- 6 teaspoons Sugar
-
-
-

-
-

  1 dash Salt

  ½ teaspoon Baking powder

  2 teaspoons Vegetable oil

  1 teaspoon Vanilla extract

  ½ teaspoon Ground cinnamon

- ¼ teaspoon Ground nutmeg
- ⅛ teaspoon Ground allspice
- 2 tablespoons Raisins
- 1 cup Finally shredded zucchini unpeeled

Combine all ingredients except raisins and zucchini. Blend until smooth. Pour mixture into a bowl. Stir zucchini and raisins into egg mixture.

Preheat a nonstick skillet or griddle over medium high heat. Drop batter onto griddle with a large spoon, making 4-inch cakes. Turn fritters carefully when edges appear dry.

21. Leek fritters

Yield: 4 Serving

Ingredient

- 4 cups Chopped leeks; (about 2 pounds)
- 1 tablespoon Vegetable oil
- 1 tablespoon Butter
- 2 cups Chopped sorrel
- 2 Eggs
-
-
-

-
-
    - ¼ cup Flour
    - ¼ teaspoon Dried lemon peel
    - ¼ teaspoon Sweet Curry Powder
    - ¼ teaspoon White pepper
    - ½ teaspoon Salt
- Sour cream

Sauté leeks in the oil and butter for about 7 minutes, until they are cooked, but not browned

Add sorrel and cook another 7 minutes, or so, until wilted. When cool, whisk together the eggs, flour, and seasonings. Add to leeks.

In a sauté pan, heat about ¼ cup vegetable oil. Ladle in enough leek mixture to make a 2-½"-3" pancake. Cook 2-3 minutes on the first side, until lightly brown, turn, and cook about 2 minutes on the second side.

Drain on paper towels and serve.

22. Lentil fritters and beet Vinaigrette

Yield: 4 Serving

Ingredient

- ¼ pound Red lentils; cooked
- 1 tablespoon Chopped fresh dill
- 1 teaspoon Paprika
- ½ teaspoon Salt
- ¾ pounds Red potatoes; peeled
-
-
-

-
-
    - Olive oil; for frying
    - ¼ pounds Beet greens; stems removed
    - 1 tablespoon Balsamic vinegar
    - ½ teaspoon Stone-ground mustard
    - ½ teaspoon Capers
- Salt
- Freshly ground black pepper
- 3 tablespoons Extra virgin olive oil

Place the lentil mash in a bowl, stir in the dill, paprika, and ½ teaspoon salt. Grate the potatoes into the bowl and stir to blend.

Form the lentil mixture into half-dollar-sized fritters and fry in a thin layer of oil until browned

Dressing: Place the vinegar, mustard, capers, salt, and pepper in a small bowl. Whisk in the olive oil until blended. Parboil the beet greens in salted water until wilted. Serve

23. Eggplant fritter

Yield: 4 Serving

Ingredient

- 1 small Eggplant
- 1 teaspoon Vinegar
- 1 Egg
- $\frac{1}{4}$ teaspoon Salt
- 3 tablespoons Flour
- $\frac{1}{2}$ teaspoon Baking powder

Peel & slice eggplant. Cook until tender in boiling, salted water. Add vinegar & let stand for a minute to prevent discoloration.

Drain eggplant & mash. Beat in other ingredients & drop from spoon into hot fat, turning the fritters so they brown evenly. Drain well on paper towels & keep warm.

Finely chopped onions, parsley, etc., may be added.

24. Curried carrot fritters

Yield: 1 Serving

Ingredient

- ½ cup Flour
- 1 Egg, slightly beaten
- 1 teaspoon Curry powder
- ½ pound Carrots
- ¼ teaspoon Salt
- ½ cup Flat beer
- 1 Egg white

Combine flour, salt, egg, 1 tablespoon of vegetable oil and beer to make a smooth batter.

Stir in curry powder. Beat egg white until stiff and fold it into batter. Gently fold in carrots.

Drop large spoonfuls of mixture into 375-degree vegetable oil, and cook about one minute on each side.

25. Fried pea fritters

Yield: 4 Serving

Ingredient

- 2 cups Field peas (cooked)
- 1 cup Flour
- 2 teaspoons Baking powder
- 1 teaspoon Pepper
- ½ teaspoon Salt
- 1 tablespoon Curry powder

- 2 Eggs

- 1½ cup Milk

Mix all dry ingredients. Beat eggs and milk. Add to the flour mixture. Gently stir in cooked peas.

Drop from spoon into ¾ inch hot fat. Fry until light brown. Serves 4 to 5

26. Stuffed potato fritters

Yield: 1 Serving

Ingredient

- ¼ cup Corn oil
- 3 mediums (1-1/2 cups) onions; chopped
- 1 pounds Ground beef
- 1 teaspoon Salt
- ½ teaspoon Pepper
- 3 pounds Potatoes; cooked and mashed

-
- 1 Egg; beaten

   1 teaspoon Salt; or to taste

- ½ teaspoon Ground cinnamon
- ½ teaspoon Pepper
- 1 cup Matzoh meal

Heat oil in a skillet & stir-fry onions over moderate heat until golden. Add beef, salt, & pepper, & stir-fry until mixture is dry & all liquid has evaporated. Add mashed potatoes.

Shape ½ cup of potato dough into a circle in palm of hand. Place 1 generous stuffing in center & fold the dough over into a slightly flattened sausage shape

Pan-fry in oil over moderate heat until brown on both sides.

27. Mushroom fritters

Yield: 6 Serving

Ingredient

- 1 cup All-purpose flour
- 1 12 oz can of beer
- 1½ teaspoon Salt
- ¼ teaspoon Black pepper
- 1 teaspoon Paprika
- 1 pounds Mushrooms
- Lemon juice

-
- Salt

    4 cups Oil for frying

Prepare batter by blending all but mushrooms, salt, and lemon till smooth.

Sprinkle mushrooms with a little lemon juice and salt.

Dip a mushroom in the batter and drop into hot oil cooking till golden. Keep mushrooms that are already cooked on a sheet lined with absorbent paper in a low oven.

28. Onion bhajiyas / onion fritters

Yield: 6 Serving

Ingredient

- 1½ cup lentil or chick-pea flour
- 1 teaspoon Salt or to taste
- 1 pinch Baking soda
- 1 tablespoon Ground rice
- Pinch cumin/chili powder/coriander
- 1 To 2 fresh green chili peppers

-
- 2 large Onions, sliced into rings and separated

    Oil for deep frying

Sieve the flour and add salt, baking soda, ground rice, cumin, coriander, chili powder and green chili peppers; mix well. Now add the onions and mix thoroughly.

Gradually add water and keep mixing until a soft thick batter is formed.

Heat the oil and fry fritters gently to ensure that the batter at the center stays soft, while the outside turns golden brown and crisp. This should take about 12 to 12 minutes each batch.

Drain fritters on paper towels.

29. Pakora

Yield: 12 Serving

Ingredient

- 1 cup Chickpea flour
- ½ cup Unbleached all-purpose flour
- ½ teaspoon Baking soda
- ¾ teaspoon Cream of tartar
- ¼ teaspoon Sea salt
- 1 teaspoon Cumin powder & Coriander powder
- 1 teaspoon Turmeric & Cayenne pepper
- 2 tablespoons Lemon juice

-
- 1 cup Sliced potatoes
- 1 cup Cauliflower florets
- 1 cup Chopped bell pepper

Blend flours, baking soda, cream of tartar, salt and spices.

Gradually whisk in water and lemon juice to make a smooth batter the consistency of heavy cream. Set aside.

Dip vegetables in batter to coat. Immerse in hot oil, turning to cook evenly, until golden brown, about 5 minutes. Remove with a slotted spoon and drain on absorbent paper.

30. Parsnip and carrot fritters

Yield: 4 Serving

Ingredient

- 225 grams Parsnip; grated
- 2 mediums Carrots; grated
- 1 Onion; grated
- 3 tablespoons Fresh snipped chives
- Salt and freshly ground black pepper
- 2 mediums Eggs
- ½ package Pork Sausages

- 100 grams Strong Cheddar cheese
- 40 grams Plain flour
- 2 tablespoons Fresh chopped parsley

Mix together the parsnips, carrots, onion, chives, seasoning and one egg, until well blended. Divide into four, flattening out into rough pancakes.

Heat a large frying pan and cook the sausages for 10 minutes, turning occasionally until golden.

Meanwhile, add the pancakes to the pan and fry for 3 minutes on each side until golden

Mix together the remaining ingredients to form a firm paste and roll into a large log shape. Slice into four. Chop the sausages and divide between the fritters. Top each with a cheese slice.

Place under the preheated grill and cook for 5-8 minutes until bubbling and melted. Serve immediately garnished with chives and chutneys.

31. Pomme frites/patatine fritters

Yield: 4 Serving

Ingredient

- 1 pounds Russet potatoes
- 4 quarts Virgin olive oil
- Salt and pepper

Cut potatoes into finger-sized slices of equal size and place in new cold water.

Heat oil to 385 F in a pot double the volume of oil

Add potatoes one handful at a time and cook until golden brown. Remove and drain on paper, season with salt and pepper and serve with mayonnaise

32. Potato and walnut fritters

Yield: 4 Serving

Ingredient

- 2 Boiling potatoes
- Salt
- 2 large Eggs
- ½ cup Chopped walnuts
- Freshly ground pepper
- 5 cups Vegetable oil, for deep frying

Heat oil for deep frying to 360 degrees

Make fritters from mixture but do not crowd them in oil. Fry 23 minutes or until golden brown on all sides.

Transfer to a tray lined with paper towels.

33.Pumpkin fritters

Yield: 1 Serving

Ingredient

- 4 cups Cooked mashed pumpkin
- 2 Eggs
- 1 cup Flour
- 1 pinch Salt
- 1 teaspoon Baking powder
- 2 tablespoons heaped of sugar
-
-

- 250 milliliters Sugar
- 500 milliliters Water
- 500 milliliters Milk
- 30 milliliters Margarine
- 20 milliliters Corn starch mixed with water

Combine all ingredients, making a soft batter and fry spoonfuls in shallow oil till both sides are lightly browned.

Drain on paper and serve warm with cinnamon sugar or caramel sauce.

34. Spinach fritters

Yield: 4 Serving

Ingredient

- 1 pounds Fresh spinach or other
- Vegetable of your choice
- 3 large Eggs
- 2 tablespoons Milk
- 1 teaspoon Salt
-
-

½ teaspoon Pepper

2 tablespoons Minced onion

- 1 tablespoon Chopped celery
- 1 tablespoon Flour
- Cooking oil

Rinse the spinach well, drain and chop it fine.

Separate the eggs and beat the whites until they stand in soft peaks.

Combine the egg yolks with the milk, salt, pepper, onion, celery and flour. Fold in the beaten egg whites and the spinach, mixing well.

Shape into 8 3 inch patties and Fry in cooking oil until browned.

35. Deep fried tofu fritters

Yield: 4 Serving

Ingredient

- 50 grams Self-rising flour
- Salt and freshly ground pepper
- Vegetable oil for frying
- 285g tofu; cut into chunks
- 2 tablespoons Caster sugar
- 2 tablespoons Red wine vinegar
-
-

300 grams Mixed berries

2 Shallots; finely diced

Make the salsa. Place the vinegar and sugar in a pan and gently heat to dissolve the sugar. Add the berries and shallots and poach gently for 10 minutes until softened. Allow to cool.

Make the batter, place the flour in a bowl and gradually whisk in the water.

Heat the oil in a deep pan until hot. Dip the tofu in the batter and deep fry for 1-2 minutes until the batter is crispy.

36. Tomato fritters

Yield: 16 Serving

Ingredient

- 1⅓ cup Plum tomatoes, seeded, diced
- ⅔ cup Zucchini, finely diced
- ½ cup Onion, finely chopped
- 2 tablespoons Mint leaves, chopped
- ½ cup All-purpose flour
-
-

- ¾ teaspoon Baking powder
- ½ teaspoon Salt
- ½ teaspoon Pepper
- Pinch Cinnamon
- Olive oil for frying

Combine diced tomatoes, zucchini, onion and mint in a small bowl

Combine flour, baking powder, salt & pepper and cinnamon in a medium bowl. Stir vegetables into dry ingredients.

Heat olive oil in a large non-stick skillet and drop batter by rounded tablespoonful into oil. Cook until golden brown, about 2 minutes per side.

Drain on paper towels, serve hot.

FRUIT FRITTERS

37. Dutch apple fritters

Yield: 4 Serving

Ingredient

- 8 large Apples peeled, cored
- 2 cups All-purpose flour, sifted
- 12 ounces Ale
- ½ teaspoon Salt
- Oil, lard or shortening
-

Confectioners' sugar

Slice the peeled and cored apples or cut into rounds at ⅓ inch thick.

Combine ale, flour and salt with whisk, until mixture is smooth then Dip apple slices in mixture.

Fry in deep fat or in 1 inch of oil in heavy skillet at 370° frying temperature. Drain

38. Apple-orange fritters

Yield: 18 Serving

Ingredient

- 1 cup Milk
- 1 Orange, rind and juice
- 1 Egg, beaten
- 1 cup Apples, coarse chopped
- 4 tablespoons Margarine
- 3 cups Cake flour

- ¼ cup Sugar
- 2 teaspoons Baking powder
- ½ teaspoon Salt
- 1 teaspoon Vanilla

Beat egg. In a mixing bowl, combine the milk, egg and melted margarine. Add the orange juice, rind, chopped apples and vanilla.

Sift together the flour, salt, baking powder. Stir into milk mixture with a spoon until blended.

Preheat oil in a skillet to 350~. Drop off end of tablespoon into hot oil. Fry to a golden brown. Turn so they brown evenly. Allow to cool.

39. Banana fritters in tempura batter

Yield: 1 Serving

Ingredient

- 5 Bananas
- Flour for dredging bananas
- Veg oil for deep frying
- 1 Egg
- 125 milliliters Flour sifted
- 1/2 tsp. baking soda
- Honey

Mix up the batter ingredients with a whip until somewhat frothy.

Cut the bananas into 1 inch / $2\frac{1}{2}$ cm chunks. Roll them around in the flour until lightly coated.

Dip a few banana pieces into the batter and fry them until golden. Drain on paper towels. Do in small batches until they're all done.

Heat honey in saucepan until liquid and hot; pour this over the bananas.

40. Apricot fritters

Yield: 8 Serving

Ingredient

- 12 smalls Apricots
- 12 Whole almonds
- 2 tablespoons White rum
- ½ cup Unbleached all-purpose flour
- ½ cup Cornstarch
- 3 tablespoons Sugar
- ½ teaspoon Salt

- ½ teaspoon Cinnamon

- ½ teaspoon Baking powder
- ½ cup Water; plus
- 1 tablespoon Water
- 3 tablespoons Melted butter
- 1½ quart Vegetable oil; for frying
- Confectioners' sugar

Place the apricots in a bowl and sprinkle the slit sides with the rum.

For the batter, combine the dry ingredients in a bowl and whisk in the water, then the melted butter.

With a fork, dip the apricots into the batter until deep golden and the apricots are cooked

41. Benya banana fritters

Yield: 1 Serving

Ingredient

- 1 Package of yeast
- 1 cup Hot water
- Sugar
- 10 Very soft bananas
- 3 tablespoons Cinnamon
- 2 tablespoons Nutmeg
- 2½ pounds Flour

- 1½ pounds Sugar

    Grated rind of orange

- ¼ teaspoon Salt

Add yeast to hot water and sprinkle in a little sugar. Cover and let stand to start rising process.

Mash bananas thoroughly in large mixing bowl with yeast. Add cinnamon, nutmeg, flour, sugar, grated orange rind and salt. Mix thoroughly and let stand overnight. Mixture will rise and triple in amount.

Drop by spoonfuls in deep fat; fry until brown. Serve either hot or cold

42. Langoustine and banana fritter

Yield: 1 Serving

Ingredient

- 4 Plump langoustines
- 1 Banana
- 8 ounces Corn flour
- 8 ounces Plain flour
- 1 ounce Baking powder
- 3½ tablespoon Tomato ketchup

- ¼ pint Vinegar

    Salt and pepper

Put the corn flour, flour, salt and pepper in a mixing bowl. Add the ketchup and vinegar and whisk to a smooth paste. Add the baking powder.

Heat a pan or an electric fryer to 175-180C.

Peel the langoustines and clean out the intestines. Split the langoustines in to and place a piece of banana down the centre. Secure together with a cocktail stick. Dip in the batter and deep fry.

43. Canned peach fritters

Yield: 4 -5 serving

Ingredient

- 1 can (29 oz) sliced peaches
- 1 cup Flour-sifted BEFORE measuring
- ½ teaspoon Salt
- 1 teaspoon Baking powder
- 2 Eggs; beaten
- 1 tablespoon Melted shortening

- ½ cup Whole milk

    Vegetable oil

Drain peaches and sprinkle lightly with flour. Sift flour with salt and baking powder. Add well-beaten eggs, melted shortening and milk. Mix well.

With a long-handles fork, dip fruit into batter. Allow excess batter to drain off.

Lower fruit into hot oil (375) and fry 2-3 minutes or until light brown

Drain on paper towels. Sprinkle with powdered sugar.

44. Caribbean pineapple fritters

Yield: 1 Serving

Ingredient

- 2 cups Fresh pineapple; cut in chunks
- 1 Habanero chile pepper; seeded and minced
- 5 Chives; finely minced
- 1 Onion; minced
- 2 Cloves garlic; mashed & minced

- 8 Green onions; minced
- ½ teaspoon Turmeric

    1¼ cup Flour
- ½ cup Milk; or more
- ½ cup Vegetable oil; for frying
- 2 Eggs; beaten
- Salt and pepper
- Pineapple rings; for garnish

Mix first seven ingredients; set aside.

Combine flour, milk, eggs, and salt and pepper together and beat well with an electric mixer.. After 4 hours, combine fruit with batter.

Heat the vegetable oil in a deep skillet. Drop batter in by spoonfuls and fry for about 5 minutes, or until they are golden brown.

Remove fritters and drain on paper towels. Serve cold

45. Elderberry fritters

Yield: 4 Serving

Ingredient

- 200 grams Flour (1 3/4 cups)
- 2 Eggs
- 1/8 litre Milk (1/2 cup plus 1/2 Tbsp)
- Small pinch salt
- 16 Elderberry blossoms with stems
- Sugar for dusting
- 750 grams Lard or shortening for frying

With a whisk, mix the flour, eggs, salt, and milk into a pancake batter. Rinse the elderberry blossoms several times, and then pat dry with paper towel.

Briefly dip the blossoms into the dough, and then deep fry until golden brown. Dust with sugar and serve.

-
-

46.Fruit and vegetable fritters

Yield: 1 Serving

Ingredient

- 1 cup All-purpose flour
- 1 teaspoon Baking powder
- 14 teaspoons Salt
- 2 large Eggs
- 2 teaspoons Sugar

- ⅔ cup Milk
- 1 teaspoon Salad oil
- ½ teaspoon Lemon juice

    Mixed fruit

    Mixed vegetables

Sift flour, baking powder and salt together. Beat the eggs until light and fluffy. Add sugar, milk, oil and dash of lemon juice; add flour mixture and stir only long enough to dampen. Add a dash of cinnamon to the flour when making fruit fritters.

FRUITS: Apples: Peel, core and cut in ½-inch slices. Bananas: Cut into chunks and sprinkle with lemon juice and sugar. Use canned peaches, pineapple etc. by draining; sprinkle very lightly with flour before dipping into batter.

VEGETABLES: Cut into equal-sized pieces to keep frying time approximately the same.

Heat oil in deep skillet and Cook fritters until delicately brown, then drain on paper towels.

-
-

47. Fruit fritters with lemon-bourbon sauce

Yield: 32 Serving

Ingredient

- ¾ cup Flour, all-purpose
- ½ teaspoon Baking powder
- 1 Egg, beaten
- 1 tablespoon Butter or margarine, melted
- ⅓ cup Sugar

  1 tablespoon Cornstarch

- ¾ cup Water

- 2 tablespoons Butter or margarine

- 1 teaspoon Vanilla

- 4 Apples, 4 Pears, 4 Bananas

- ¼ cup Bourbon

- Lemon rind & 4 teaspoons Lemon juice

Sift together flour, sugar and baking powder.

Combine egg, water, butter and vanilla; stir into dry ingredients until just blended.

Dip fruit slice in batter; drop into hot oil and fry until golden on both sides.

LEMON-BOURBON SAUCE: Combine sugar and cornstarch in small saucepan; stir in water. Cook, stirring constantly, until mixture boils and thickens. Stir in butter. Add bourbon, lemon rind and juice; mix well.

48. Northern spy apple fritters

-
-
-

Yield: 15 Serving

Ingredient

- ¾ cup Yellow cornmeal
- ½ cup All-purpose flour
- 2 tablespoons Baking powder
- 6 tablespoons Sugar
- 1 pinch Of salt

    1 Egg

    ½ cup Milk

- 1½ cup Vegetable oil for frying

- 1 Northern Spy apple, peeled

- 2 tablespoons Vegetable oil

- Confectioner's sugar for garnish

Combine all dry ingredients except for confectioners' sugar

Add liquid ingredients (except for 1½ cups of oil) one at a time, stirring between additions. Mix in apple. Let batter sit for 10 minutes.

Heat the oil until it crackles, not quite to the smoking point. Drop batter into the oil and remove onto a paper towel when golden brown.

Sprinkle with confectioners' sugar and serve.

49. Pineapple banana fritters

Yield: 1 Serving

Ingredient

- 1⅓ cup All-purpose flour
- 1½ teaspoon Double-acting baking powder
- 3 tablespoons Granulated sugar
- 1 teaspoon Ground ginger

    ¾ cup Chopped fresh pineapple; drained

¾ cup Chopped banana

½ cup Milk

1 large Egg; beaten lightly

Vegetable oil for deep-frying

- Confectioners' sugar for dusting the

Sift together the flour, the baking powder, the granulated sugar, the ginger, and a pinch of salt.

In a bowl combine well the pineapple, the banana, the milk, and the egg, add the flour mixture, and stir the batter until it is combined.

Drop the batter by tablespoonfuls into the oil in batches, and fry the fritters, turning them, for 1 to 1 ½ minutes, or until they are golden.

Transfer the fritters with slotted spoon to paper towels to drain and sift the confectioners' sugar over them.

-
-
-

-
-

50.Poached pear fritters

Yield: 1 Serving

Ingredient

- 1 Recipe Traditional Buttermilk Biscuits
- Vegetable oil
- 1 Bottle port
- 1 cup Water
- 1 Cinnamon stick

- 3 Whole cloves

  ½ teaspoon Nutmeg

  1 pinch Mace

  4 Pears; peeled

-
-
-

Place the ingredients in a pot and bring to a boil add pears. Boil until pears are slightly poached 15 to 20 minutes.

Once cooled, remove the pears and strain the liquids, place back in the pot and bring to a boil. Reduce by half and remove from heat. Cut the pears in quarters, removing the seeds.

Roll the dough twice the length of the pears width and as long as you can get it $\frac{1}{8}$- to $\frac{1}{4}$-inch thick. Place the pears on the dough, fold dough over top and cut with a pastry wheel. Repeat until dough and pears are all used.

Bake biscuits.

SEAFOOD RFRITTERS

51. Catfish fritters

Yield: 8 Serving

Ingredient

- 1½ cup Flour, all-purpose
- 1 teaspoon Salt pepper
- 2 mediums Eggs
- 3 tablespoons Butter, unsalted; melted, cooled
- 1 cup Milk, whole
- ½ pounds Salt codfish
- 1 each Pepper, hot; seeded

-
-
    2 each Scallions; chopped fine

    1 each Garlic cloves; crushed

- 1 tablespoon Parsley; chopped
- ½ teaspoon Thyme
- 1 each allspice berry; ground

Sift flour and salt into bowl. Beat eggs with butter and add to flour mixture. Add milk gradually, stirring only to mix. Add more milk if batter is too stiff.

Pound fish in mortar with hot pepper

Add scallions, garlic, parsley, thyme, allspice, and black pepper to taste. Stir into batter

Heat oil and fry mixture by heaping tablespoons until golden brown.

52. Codfish fritters

Yield: 14 fritters

Ingredient

- ½ pounds Dried salt cod, cooked & shredded
- Vegetable oil for deep-fat frying
- 1½ cup Unsifted all-purpose flour
- ½ teaspoon Baking powder
- ½ teaspoon Cracked black pepper
- ¼ teaspoon Salt
- 2 Large egg whites

-
-
    2 Cloves garlic, crushed

    2 tablespoons Chopped fresh cilantro leaves

In large bowl, combine flour, baking powder, cracked black pepper, and salt.

In small bowl, beat egg whites until frothy-add beaten egg whites and water to flour mixture to create a batter. Add shredded salt cod, garlic, and chopped fresh cilantro leaves; stir until well combined.

In batches, drop heaping tablespoonfuls of batter into hot oil and fry 12 minutes.

Drain on paper towels and serve warm on serving plate; garnish with cilantro.

53. Fish and crab meat fritters

Yield: 1 Serving

Ingredient

- 12 ounces Fresh or frozen cod
- 6 ounces Imitation crab meat
- 2 Eggs; beaten
- 1/2 cup flour
- 1 Green onion; finely chopped
- ½ teaspoon Finely shredded lemon peel
- 1 teaspoon Lemon juice
- 1 Cloves garlic; crushed

-
-
    - ¼ teaspoon Salt
    - ½ teaspoon Pepper
- Cooking oil

In a blender container or food processor bowl, combine fish crab, eggs, flour, onion, lemon peel, lemon juice, garlic, salt and pepper. Cover and blend until smooth.

Lightly oil skillet and heat

Spoon about ¼ cup batter onto skillet and spread to a patty 3 inches in diameter

Cook 3 minutes per side or until golden

54. cape cod clam & corn fritters

Yield: 1 Serving

Ingredient

- 2 Eggs, well beaten
- ¼ cup Clam liquid
- ¼ cup Milk
- 1 tablespoon Oil
- 1½ cup Flour
- 1 teaspoon Baking powder Salt to taste

-
-
- 1 cup Well-drained kernel corn

- ½ cup Well-drained minced clams

Beat eggs; add milk, clam liquid, oil and beat until well blended.

Stir in flour, baking powder and salt to taste. Beat until well blended. Add corn and clams. Drop by well-rounded tablespoons into hot oil. Cook until browned on both sides. Drain on paper towels.

-
-

55. Conch fritters

Yield: 50 Serving

Ingredient

- 2 pounds Conch, finely chopped
- 1 cup Lime juice
- ¼ cup Olive oil
- 1 Green bell pepper

- 1 Red bell pepper

    1 large Onion, chopped fine

    4 Eggs, beaten

    2 cups Flour

    1 teaspoon Salt
- 1 teaspoon Cajun seasoning
- 6 dashes Tabasco sauce
- 3 teaspoons Baking powder
- 5 tablespoons Margarine, melted
- Vegetable oil for frying

Have fish market put conch through tenderizer. Marinate conch in 1 cup lime juice and ¼ cup olive oil for at least 30 minutes; drain.

Mix all ingredients together. Fry in HOT vegetable oil until golden, about 3-5 minutes. Serve with red cocktail sauce ort tartar sauce.

-
-

56. Canned clam fritters

Yield: 12 Serving

Ingredient

- 1 Egg; well-beaten
- ½ teaspoon Salt
- ⅛ teaspoon Black pepper
- ⅔ cup White wheat flour
- 1 teaspoon Baking powder

¼ cup Canned clam broth or milk

1 tablespoon butter; melted

1 cup Minced canned clams; drained

Oil or clarified butter

- ¼ cup Sour cream or yogurt
- 1 teaspoon Dill; tarragon or thyme

Gently mix all ingredients together, adding the clams last. Drop 2 heaping tablespoonfuls per fritter onto a hot greased griddle or an iron skillet.

When bubbles break, turn the fritters.

Serve warm with a dollop of herbed sour cream, yogurt or tartar sauce.

57. Crab & avocado fritters

Yield: 4 Serving

Ingredient

- 2 pounds Crabmeat
- Salt
- 1 cup Diced green onions
- ¼ cup Dry breadcrumbs
- 1 medium Avocado, peeled and cut

    Corn Oil For Deep-Frying

All-Purpose Flour

Thinly slivered green onion

2 Eggs

- ½ cup Hot chili salsa

Combine crab, 1 c green onions and avocado in large bowl. Mix eggs, salsa and salt; add to crab. Mix in breadcrumbs. Form mixture into 1½ inch balls.

Pour oil into large skillet to depth of 3 inches.

Heat to 350 degrees

Dust fritters with flour. Carefully ad to oil in batches (do not crowd) and cook until golden brown, about 2 minutes per side.

Drain on paper towels. Transfer to prepared sheet and keep warm in oven until all are cooked. Garnish with green onion slivers and serve immediately

58. Crawfish fritters

Yield: 6 Serving

Ingredient

- 1 cup Crawfish tails
- ¼ cup Pimientos, chopped
- ¼ cup Green onions, chopped
- 2 cups Flour

- 1 teaspoon Baking soda
- ½ teaspoon Salt
- ½ teaspoon Liquid crab boil
- ½ cup Broth or water
- Oil for frying

Add pimientos and green onions to crawfish. Sift flour, baking soda and salt together and add to crawfish. Add broth or water and mix to make a thick batter. Cover and let rest for ½ hour.

Drop batter by spoonsful and fry until golden brown

-
-

59. Clam fritters

Yield: 4 Serving

Ingredient

- 1 pint Clams
- 1 tablespoon Baking powder
- 1½ teaspoon Salt
- 1 cup Milk

- 1 tablespoon Butter

    1¾ cup Flour, all-purpose

    1 teaspoon Parsley, chopped

    2 Eggs, beaten

    2 teaspoons Onion, grated

Combine dry ingredients. Combine eggs, milk, onion, butter, and clams. Combine with dry ingredients and stir until smooth. Drop batter by using teaspoonfuls into hot shortening at 350 degrees F and fry for 3 minutes, or until golden brown.

Drain on absorbent paper.

-
-

-
-

60. Indonesian corn shrimp fritters

Yield: 6 Serving

Ingredient

- 3 Ears of Corn scraped & coarsely chopped
- ½ pounds Medium Shrimp shelled and deveined,
- 1 teaspoon Chopped garlic
- ½ cup finely chopped shallots or: Green onions
- 1 teaspoon Ground coriander
- ¼ teaspoon Ground cumin

2 tablespoons Chopped coriander leaves

2 tablespoons Flour

1 teaspoon Salt

2 Eggs, beaten

- Peanut or vegetable oil for pan-frying
- chili sauce for dipping

IN A LARGE BOWL, combine corn, shrimp, garlic, green onions, ground coriander, cumin, coriander leaves, flour, salt and eggs. Heat a thin layer of oil in a skillet over medium-high heat. Pour $\frac{1}{4}$ cup of corn mixture into pan. Add as many as will fit into the pan with $\frac{1}{2}$-inch of space between the fritters.

Fry until golden brown and crisp; turn. Cook about 1 minute on each side. Remove and drain on paper towels. Keep warm while frying remaining fritters.

61. Italian spaghetti squash fritters

Yield: 4 Serving

Ingredient

- 2 Eggs
- ½ cup Part skim ricotta cheese
- 1 ounce Grated parmesan cheese
- 3 tablespoons Flour
- ½ teaspoon Baking powder
- 2 teaspoons Veg. oil

- ⅛ teaspoon Garlic powder
- ½ teaspoon Dried oregano
  - ¼ teaspoon Dried basil
  - 1 tablespoon Minced onion flakes
- 2 cups Cooked spaghetti

In blender container, combine all ingredients, except spaghetti. Blend until smooth. Add spaghetti

Pour mixture onto a preheated nonstick skillet or griddle sprayed with Pam. Cook over med heat until brown on both sides, turning carefully.

SAUCE: Combine one 8oz can tomato sauce, ¼ teaspoon dried oregano, ⅛ teaspoon garlic powder, ¼ teaspoon dried basil in a small sauce pan. Heat until hot and bubbly

Serve over fritters.

62. Lobster fritters

Yield: 1 Serving

Ingredient

- 1 cup Chopped lobster
- 2 Eggs
- ½ cup Milk
- 1¼ cup Flour
- 2 teaspoons Baking powder
- Salt and pepper to taste

Heat deep fat until a cube of bread browns in sixty seconds. While fat is heating, beat eggs until light. Add milk and flour sifted with baking powder, salt & pepper, and then fold in chopped lobster.

Drop by small spoonfuls into fat, fry until golden brown. Drain on brown paper in warm oven. Serve with quick lemon sauce.

63. Mussel fritters with salsa

Yield: 4 Serving

Ingredient

- 8 Green shell mussels; out of the shell
- 6 large Eggs; lightly beaten
- 50 milliliters Double cream
- 10 milliliters fish paste
- 2 tablespoons Polenta
- 50 grams Spring onions; sliced
- 400 grams Kumera; boiled then peeled

- 1 small Red onion; peeled and sliced
- 20 milliliters Fresh lime juice
- 2 Nashi; core removed and
- 30 milliliters Extra virgin olive oil

Cut the mussels into quarters then mix them in a bowl with the eggs, cream, nam pla, polenta and half the spring onion. Lastly mix in the kumera.

Mix together all the other ingredients to make the salsa, including the remaining spring onions, and leave to stand for 30 minutes.

Heat a pan and brush with oil, then make either 4 large or 8 small fritters. Cook to golden brown on one side then turn and cook the other side.

64. Octopus fritters

Yield: 8 Serving

Ingredients:

- 2 Octopus about 1 1/2 poands each
- 1 teaspoon Salt
- 2 quarts Water
- 2 quarts Ice water with ice
- 2 mediums Onions, peeled and minced
- 2 Eggs, beaten
- 1 cup Flour or more as needed

- Salt and pepper to taste
- Oil for frying

Drop the octopus into a large kettle with rapidly boiling salted water. Cook on medium-high heat for about 25 minutes. Drain and plunge into a bowl filled with ice and ice water. With a coarse brush scrape away act of the purple skin. Cut off the legs and chop fine.

Discard the heads. In a bowl mix together onions, eggs, flour and salt and pepper. Add chopped octopus, and blend well. Form mixture into $2\frac{1}{2}$ - 3 inch flat patties. Heat about $\frac{1}{2}$ inch of oil in a large heavy skillet, and fry the octopus fritters until well browned on each side. Serve immediately.

65. Shrimp fritter

Yield: 8 Serving

Ingredient

- ½ cup Milk
- ½ cup Self-rising flour
- 1 cup Raw shrimp; chopped
- 1 cup Cooked rice
- 1 Egg
- ½ cup Green onions; chopped
- Salt & pepper to taste

Mix all ingredients together. Drop by teaspoon into hot cooking oil and fry into golden brown. Make small and serve as an appetizer.

66. Oyster corn fritters

Yield: 1 Serving

Ingredient

- 2 cups Corn pulp
- 2 Egg, separated
- ¼ teaspoon Pepper
- 2 tablespoons Flour
- ½ teaspoon Salt

Canned or fresh corn may be used. To the corn pulp add the beaten egg yolks, flour and seasoning. Add the stiffly beaten egg whites and blend.

Drop by spoonfuls the size of an oyster on a hot buttered frying pan and brown. Source: Pennsylvania Dutch Cook Book - Fine Old Recipes, Culinary Arts Press, 1936.

67. Tuna fritters

Yield: 3 Serving

Ingredient

- 1 cup Flour
- 1 teaspoon Baking powder
- ½ teaspoon Salt
- 2 Eggs
- ¼ cup Milk
- 1 can Tuna, drained and flaked

- 6 1/2 or 7 oz. size
- Dried onion flakes
- Oil for frying

Sift flour, baking powder and salt into a mixing bowl. Beat the eggs well. Beat in milk. Combine liquid ingredients with dry ingredients.

Stir until all flour is moistened. Stir in the tuna. Drop by teaspoonfuls into hot oil, 375 degrees. Fry until golden on all sides. Drain on paper towels.

CHEESE FRITTERS

68. Basle cheese fritters

Yield: 1 Serving

Ingredient

- 4 Slices bread
- 1 ounce Butter
- 3 Onions
- 4 Slices Gruyere
- Paprika

Fry bread lightly on both sides in butter and arrange on a baking sheet. Pour boiling water over finely chopped onions and leave for a moment. Pour off water, and fry onions in the remains of the butter until tender.

Spread onions thinly on the bread and cover each slice with a slice of cheese.

Sprinkle with paprika and bake in a very hot oven (445 degrees F/Gas mark 8) until cheese melts. Serve at once.

69. Herb fritters with yoghurt apricot dip

Yield: 6 Serving

Ingredient

- 3 Eggs; lightly beaten
- 150 grams Mozzarella; grated
- 85 grams Freshly grated Parmesan
- 125 grams Fresh breadcrumbs
- ½ Red onion; finely chopped
- ¼ teaspoon Red chili flakes
- 2 tablespoons fresh marjoram

- 2 tablespoons Roughly chopped chives
- 5 tablespoons chopped flat leaf parsley
- 1 Handful rocket leaves; roughly chopped
- 1 Handful baby spinach leaves; chopped
- Salt and pepper & sunflower oil
- 500 gram tub Greek yoghurt
- 12 Ready-to-eat dried apricots; finely diced
- 2 Garlic cloves & Chopped fresh mint

Mix the fritter ingredients, except the oil and butter, until thick and fairly solid. Bind with breadcrumbs if damp.

Mix the sauce ingredients just before using. Pour 1cm/ $\frac{1}{2}$" oil into a frying pan, add the butter and heat until hazy.

Mold oval-shaped fritters, pressing firmly with your hand to compact it. Fry in the oil for 2-3 minutes until crisp.

70. Bern cheese fritters

Yield: 1 Serving

Ingredient

- 8 ounces Grated Gruyere cheese
- 2 Eggs
- 2½ fluid ounce Milk
- 1 teaspoon Kirsch
- Fat for frying
- 6 Slices bread

Mix grated cheese with the egg yolks, milk and Kirsch. Fold in beaten egg whites, and spread mixture on bread.

Heat fat in a large frying pan and place bread, cheese side down, in hot fat

When slices become golden brown, turn and fry briefly on the other side.

71. Bean, corn & cheddar fritters

Yield: 5 Serving

Ingredient

- ½ cup Yellow cornmeal
- ½ cup Unbleached white flour
- ½ teaspoon Baking powder
- Dash Ground cumin, cayenne, salt & chili powder
- ½ cup Milk
- 1 Egg yolk & 2 Egg whites
- 1 cup Black beans; cooked

- 1 cup Sharp Cheddar cheese
- ½ cup Fresh corn; or frozen corn kernels
- 2 tablespoons Cilantro; minced fresh
- Red bell pepper & Green chili peppers, Roasted

Stir together the cornmeal, flour, baking powder, salt, chili powder, cumin, and cayenne in a medium-size bowl.

Beat the milk with the egg yolk, and add it to the dry ingredients, mixing well. Stir in the beans, cheese, corn, cilantro, red pepper, and green chilies. Gently fold in the egg whites.

Heat the ½ cup oil in a 10-inch skillet over medium-high heat. Spoon in about ¼ cup of batter for each fritter and fry until golden brown.

72. Mozzarella fritters and spaghetti

Yield: 2 Serving

Ingredient

- 2 Garlic cloves
- 1 small Bunch fresh parsley & 3 Salad onions
- 225 grams Lean minced pork
- Freshly grated Parmesan & Smoked mozzarella
- 150 grams Spaghetti or tagliatelle
- 100 milliliters Hot beef stock
- 400 gram can chopped tomatoes
- 1 pinch Sugar & 1 dash Soy sauce

- Salt and pepper
- 1 Egg & 1 tablespoon Olive oil
- 75 milliliters Milk
- 50 grams Plain flour; plus extra for dusting

Mix together the garlic, salad onions, garlic, Parmesan, parsley and plenty of salt and pepper. Shape into eight firm balls. Heat the oil in a large pan and cook the meatballs. Pour in the stock.

Cook the chopped tomatoes, sugar, salt and pepper and add into the meatballs

Beat the oil, milk, flour and a little salt into the yolk to make a thick, smooth batter. Thinly slice the mozzarella, and then dust in the flour. Add egg yolks and fold in whisked egg whites.

Dip the floured mozzarella slices in the batter and cook for two minutes on each side until crisp and golden.

73. Emmenthal cheese fritters

Yield: 1 Person

Ingredient

- 1 large Slice bread
- 1 Slice ham
- 1 tablespoon Butter
- 1 Slice Emmenthal cheese
- Salt, Pepper
- 1 Egg

Lightly toast the bread. Fry the ham briefly, place on bread, cover with cheese and season. Place in fairly hot oven and allow cheese to melt, or in covered frying pan on top of the cooker. At the last moment, top cheese with a fried egg.

74. Cornmeal cheddar fritters

Yield: 1 Serving

Ingredient

- 1 cup Cornmeal
- 1 cup Grated sharp Cheddar
- ½ cup Grated onion
- ¼ cup Minced red bell pepper
- 1 teaspoon Salt
- Cayenne, to taste
- ¾ cup Boiling water

- Vegetable oil for frying

- Louisiana-style hot sauce, for example Crystal brand

In a bowl combine cornmeal, Cheddar, onion, bell pepper, salt, and cayenne.

Stir in boiling water and mix thoroughly. In a deep heavy pan or deep fryer heat 3 inches of vegetable oil to 350 F. Drop 6 spoonfuls of the batter into the oil and fry for 2-3 minutes or until golden brown.

75. Camembert fritters

Yield: 10 Serving

Ingredient

- 3 tablespoons Butter/margerine
- 3 tablespoons All-purpose flour
- 1 cup Milk
- 4 ounces Camembert Cheese
- Salt to taste
- Cayenne pepper to taste
- 1 large Egg

- 1 tablespoon Butter/margarine
- ½ cup Fine bread crumbs

Melt the butter in a heavy saucepan over med. heat. Quickly blend in the flour. Add the milk gradually, stirring thoroughly. Bring to a boil, add the cheese to the sauce and stir until it has melted. Add salt and cayenne pepper to taste.

Spread the mixture ¾ inch thick on a baking sheet. Cut the cheese mixture into squares.

Beat the eggs with the water. Roll the cheese pieces in the bread crumbs, and then dip them in the egg mixture. Roll them in the crumbs again, and shake off any excess crumbs.

Drop the cheese pieces a few at a time into the oil. Fry just until they are golden brown.

76. Cauliflower-cheddar fritters

Yield: 24 Serving

Ingredient

- 1½ cup All-purpose flour
- 2 teaspoons Baking powder
- ½ teaspoon Salt
- 2 cups Diced cauliflower
- 1 cup shredded Cheddar cheese
- 1 tablespoon Diced onion
- 1 large Egg
- 1 cup Milk

- Vegetable oil

Combine the first 3 ingredients in a large bowl; stir in cauliflower, cheese and onion.

Whisk together egg and milk. Add to flour mixture, whisking just until moistened.

Pour vegetable oil to a depth of 2 inches into a Dutch oven; heat to 375 degrees F. Drop dough by rounded tablespoonfuls into oil, and fry 1 minute on each side or until fritters are golden brown. Drain well on paper towels, and serve immediately.

77.Cheese stuffed potato fritters

Yield: 5 Serving

Ingredient

- 2 pounds Baking potatoes, cooked
- ⅓ cup Butter, softened
- 5 Egg yolk
- 2 tablespoons Parsley
- 1 teaspoon Salt
- ½ teaspoon Pepper
- Pinch Nutmeg
- 4 ounce mozzarella cheese
- All-purpose flour
- 2 large Eggs, lightly beaten
- 1½ cup Italian bread crumbs

Combine potatoes and butter in a large mixing bowl; beat at medium speed with electric mixer until smooth. Add yolks and next 4 ingredients, stirring well. Divide potato mixture into 10 portions. Wrap each portion around a slice of cheese; shaping into an oval.

Lightly dust each with flour; dip in beaten egg and dredge in Italian Bread crumbs. Refrigerate 20 minutes.

Pour oil to a depth of 4 inches in a Dutch oven Heat to 340 degrees. Fry fritters a few at a time, 8 minutes, turning once.

78. Pear and cheddar fritters

Yield: 1 Serving

Ingredient

- 4 mediums Bartlett pears; peeled
- 16 slices Sharp cheddar cheese
- ½ cup All-purpose flour
- 2 large Eggs; beaten to blend
- 2 cups Fresh white breadcrumbs

Cut 3 thin vertical slices from opposite sides of each pear; discard cores.

Alternating pear and cheese slices, place 2 cheese slices between 3 pear slices for each of 8 fritters. Holding each cheese-pear sandwich firmly together, coat lightly with flour, then eggs, then breadcrumbs, coating completely and pressing crumbs to adhere.

Pour oil into heavy large skillet to depth of 1 inch and heat to 350F. Cook fritters in batches until golden, turning with slotted spoon, about 2 minutes per side. Drain on paper towels.

79. Ricotta and chestnut fritters with bagna cauda

Yield: 4 Serving

Ingredient

- 1 cup Fresh ricotta
- 3 large Eggs
- ½ cup Parmigiano-Reggiano cheese
- ¼ cup Chestnut flour
- 1 cup Finely-chopped roasted chestnuts
- 1 can Anchovy filets
- 6 Garlic cloves; finely chopped
- ½ cup Extra-virgin olive oil
- 6 tablespoons Unsalted butter
- 1 quart Pure olive oil

In a large mixing bowl place the ricotta cheese, 2 eggs and ½ cup Parmigiano-Reggiano and blend well. With your hands mix in the chestnut flour until a smooth cookie-like dough forms

In a small bowl beat the remaining egg. Take a small amount of the ricotta mixture and make a 2-inch ball. Carefully cover the ball with the beaten egg and while still wet, dredge in chopped chestnuts

Meanwhile combine the anchovies with their juices, garlic and ½ cup olive oil in a small sauce pan and stir over medium heat.

Mash the anchovies to a paste. Stir in the butter 1 tablespoon at a time until melted and smooth

Fry the ricotta balls in hot oil until golden brown

80. Waadtland cheese fritters

Yield: 1 Serving

Ingredient

- 4 Slices toast, each 1 3/8 inches thick
- 2½ fluid ounce White wine
- 5½ ounce Gruyere cheese, grated
- 1 Egg
- Paprika
- Pepper

Moisten the slices of toast with a little of the wine and arrange on a baking sheet. Mix the rest of the wine with the cheese, egg and spices to a fairly thick paste and spread on the toast.

Sprinkle with more paprika and pepper. Bake briefly in a very hot oven (445 degrees F/Gas mark 8) until cheese begins to melt, serve at once.

MEATS & POULTRY FRITTERS

81. Chicken fritters

Yield: 6 Serving

Ingredient

- 20 -minutes preparation time
- 2 cups Chicken; finely chopped cooked
- 1 teaspoon Salt
- 2 teaspoons Minced fresh parsley
- 1 tablespoon Lemon juice

- 1 cup Dry mustard
- 1 cup White wine vinegar
- 2 Egg; beaten minutes cooking time
- 1¼ cup Flour
- 2 teaspoons Baking powder
- ⅔ cup Milk
- ¾ cup Honey
- ¼ teaspoon Salt

In a large bowl, toss chicken with salt, parsley, and lemon juice. Set aside for 15 minutes. In another large bowl, combine flour, baking powder, egg, and milk. Stir to blend well.

Add flour mixture to chicken and mix well.

Drop batter by tablespoons into hot oil and fry in batches without crowding for 2 minutes, until golden brown. Drain on paper towels and serve with honey mustard for dipping.

Prepare Honey mustard directions

82. Chunky beef fritters

Yield: 5 Serving

Ingredient

- 2 pounds Cooked Unseasoned Roast Beef
- 6 tablespoons Milk
- 1 tablespoon Unbleached All-purpose Flour
- 3 each Large Eggs, Beaten
- 1½ cup Self-Rising Flour
- 4 teaspoons Salt
- ¼ teaspoon Pepper

Combine milk and flour; stir into eggs. Combine self-rising flour, salt and pepper.

Dip roast beef chunks in egg mixture and dredge in flour mixture.

Fry in hot deep fat until browned and heated through. Drain on absorbent paper towels and serve hot.

83. Egg fritters with string beans and macaroni

Yield: 6 Serving

Ingredient

- 1 pounds String beans, boiled
- ½ pounds Macaroni or ziti
- ¾ cup Bread crumbs, unflavored
- ½ teaspoon Garlic, finely chopped

- Chopped parsley
- Marinara sauce
- 6 tablespoons Parmesan, grated
- 6 Eggs, beaten
- Salt/pepper
- Oil for frying

Add bread crumbs, cheese, parsley, salt, pepper, and garlic to eggs. Mix thoroughly to form a batter. Heat oil to medium high, when hot, a drop of batter should stiffen and float to the surface. Put in batter a teaspoonful at a time. Do not crowd.

When fritters have puffed up, turn them until they form a golden crust.

Combine string beans, macaroni and marinara sauce in a large serving bowl.

84. Fresh corn & sausage fritters

Yield: 24 Serving

Ingredient

- 1 cup All-purpose Flour, sifted
- 1 teaspoon Baking Powder
- 1 teaspoon Salt
- $\frac{1}{8}$ teaspoon Pepper
- $\frac{1}{4}$ teaspoon Paprika
- 1 cup Sausage, cooked and crumbled
- 1 cup Fresh Corn off the cob
- 2 Egg Yolks, beaten

- 2 tablespoons Milk
- 2 Egg Whites, beaten stiff
- Oil, for frying

Sift flour, baking powder, and spices together in a mixing bowl. Add sausage, corn, egg yolks, and milk; mix until blended. Fold in stiffly beaten egg whites.

Drop by heaping teaspoonfuls into oil heated to 360 - 365 degrees.

Cook 3 to 5 minutes, turning to brown on all sides. Drain on paper towels.

85. Hot dog corn fritters

Yield: 6 grandsons

Ingredient

- 6 Eggs; separated
- 12 ounces corn with pimiento
- 6 Hot dogs
- ½ cup All-purpose flour
- ½ teaspoon Salt
- 1 tablespoon Cooking sherry

Beat the eggs yolks until they are light and fluffy; add the corn, the diced hot dogs, flour, salt and sherry. Mix very well. Beat the egg whites until they stand in peaks. Fold the egg whites into the hot dog mixture, taking care not to lose the air.

Fry on a hot, lightly greased griddle as you would pancakes, using about ¼ cup of the mixture per cake. Serve at once, piping hot.

86. Korean meat fritters

Yield 4 Serving

Ingredient

- 2 pounds Sirloin tip steak
- 3 Sprigs green onion, minced
- 2 tablespoons Sesame seed oil
- 2 teaspoons Sesame seeds
- ½ cup Soy sauce
- 1 Clove garlic, minced
- 1 Dash of black pepper

- 5 Eggs

Combine all other ingredients except eggs and soak meat in sauce for one hour.

Flour meat and dip in slightly beaten egg, and fry over medium heat until brown. Serve hot with sauce.

Sauce: 2 tbsp. soy sauce 1 tsp. chopped green onion 1 tsp. sesame seeds 1 tsp. vinegar 1 tsp. sugar Mix all ingredients together.

87. Parmesan and mozzarella fritters

Yield: 4 Serving

Ingredient

- 1 Clove garlic; chopped
- 2 Mature mozzarella; grated
- 1 small Egg; beaten
- Few leaves of fresh basil
- 70 grams Parmesan; grated
- 2 tablespoons plain flour
- Salt and pepper

Mix the mozzarella, garlic, basil, parmesan and seasoning and bind with beaten egg. Add some flour, shape and rest in the fridge for approximately 30 minutes.

Lightly coat with flour before frying

The mix should be fairly soft, because it firms up after it has rested in the fridge for the required time. The oil in the frying pan should not be too hot otherwise the fritters will burn on the outside and will be cold in the middle.

DESSERT FRITTERS

88. Chocolate-covered pecan fritters

Yield: 4 dozen

Ingredient

- 2 packs Vanilla caramels; 6 oz. ea.
- 2 tablespoons Milk, evaporated
- 2 cups Pecan halves
- 8 ounces Milk choc. bar; broken into squares
- ⅓ Paraffin bar; broken into pieces

Combine caramels and milk in top of double boiler; heat until caramels melts, stirring constantly. Beat with wooden spoon until creamy; stir in pecans. Drop by teaspoonfuls onto buttered waxed paper; let stand 15 minutes.

Combine chocolate and paraffin in top of double boiler; heat until melted and smooth, stirring occasionally.

Using a toothpick, dip each fritter into chocolate mixture

Place on waxed paper to cool.

89. Choux fritters

Yield: 1 Serving

Ingredient

- ½ cup Butter or margarine
- 1 cup Boiling water
- ¼ teaspoon Salt
- 1¾ cup Flour
- 4 Eggs
- 4 cups Vegetable oil; (12 oz)
- Granulated sugar

Combine butter, boiling water, salt, and flour in a saucepan over moderate heat. Beat mixture vigorously until it leaves sides of pan and forms a ball. Remove from heat and cool slightly. Spoon into a mixer or food processor with a steel blade, and add eggs one at a time, beating well after each addition. When all eggs have been added and mixture is thick, it should hold its shape when lifted with a spoon.

Dip a tablespoon first in hot oil, then in batter.

Carefully drop tablespoonfuls of batter into hot oil and cook until brown on all sides. Remove from oil with a slotted spoon and drain on paper towels.

90. Christmas pudding fritters

Yield: 1 Serving

Ingredient

- 25 gram Self raising flour
- 125 milliliter Beer
- 125 milliliter Milk
- 125 milliliter Cold water
- 1 Left over Christmas pudding
- 1 Plain flour

- 1 Deep fryer with oil

Combine the first four ingredients to make a batter. Set aside for 20 minutes.

Heat the deep fryer to 180C.

Cut the pudding into cubes or fingers, roll through the flour and then dip in the batter. deep fry until golden.

Drain on kitchen towel and serve.

91. Cinnamon fritters

Yield: 1 Serving

Ingredient

- 1 cup Hot water
- ⅓ cup Shortening
- 2 cups Flour
- ½ cup Sugar
- 1 tablespoon Cinnamon
- Salt

- 2 teaspoons Baking powder
- Oil for deep frying
- $\frac{1}{4}$ Cinnamon
- $\frac{1}{2}$ cup Castor sugar

Melt the shortening in the hot water. Stir in the flour, sugar, cinnamon, salt & baking powder. Mix well. Roll into a ball & chill the dough for at least 1 hour. Heat 1" vegetable oil to 375 in a deep fryer or skillet. Break off small lumps of dough & roll into balls.

Deep fry for 3-4 minutes until brown

Lift out of hot oil with slotted spoon. Drain on paper towels & cool for a few minutes on rack. Mix cinnamon & sugar together in a bowl. Roll warm cinnamon fritters in the sugar mixture to coat them completely. Serve warm.

92. French fritters

Yield: 1 Serving

Ingredient

- 2 Eggs; separated
- ⅔ cup Milk
- 1 cup Flour; sifted
- ½ teaspoon Salt
- 1 tablespoon Butter; melted
- 2 tablespoons Lemon juice
- 1 Lemon; rind grated

- 2 tablespoons Sugar
- 4 Apples or oranges, pineapple
- Figs or pears

Sprinkle fruit slices of your choice with the lemon rind and sugar and let stand for 2 to 3 hours. Drain and dip in the thin Fritter Batter.

Batter: Beat together with mixer, egg yolks, milk, flour, salt butter and lemon juice. Fold in the stiffly beaten egg whites.

Fry in deep fat 375

Drain and serve hot with 10xsugar, or a sweet syrup or sauce.

93. Maple fritters

Yield: 24 Fritters

Ingredient

- 3 each Eggs
- 1 tablespoon Cream
- ½ teaspoon Salt
- 2 cups Milk
- 2 teaspoons Baking powder
- 4 cups Flour

Combine baking powder and salt with flour and add milk. Beat eggs and cream together and stir into flour mixture. Drop by tablespoons into hot fat, heated to 370*F and fry until done, about 5 minutes. Serve with warm maple syrup.

94. Rum cherry fritters

Yield: 6 Serving

Ingredient

- ½ cup All-purpose flour
- 2 tablespoons Confectioner's sugar
- ¼ teaspoon Salt
- 1 pounds Cherries with stems
- Confectioner's sugar
- 2 Eggs; separated
- 2 tablespoons Rum

- ½ cup Clarified butter
- ½ cup Vegetable oil

In a medium bowl, mix together the flour, egg yolks, 2 T confectioner's sugar, rum and salt to form a smooth batter. Cover and let stand 1 to 2 hours.

Beat the egg whites until they are stiff and fold them into the batter.

Heat the butter and vegetable oil in a large frying pan to 360 degrees F., then turn the heat to low.

Dip the cherries into the batter and stand them up into the hot oil

Fry for 3 minutes, or until they are golden brown

Remove the cherries. Dip them into the confectioner's sugar and serve.

95. Suvganiot

Yield: 20 Or 25

Ingredient

- 1 cup Warm water
- 1 pack Dry yeast
- 1 tablespoon Sugar
- 4 cups All-purpose flour
- 1 cup Warm milk
- 1 tablespoon Unsalted butter (melted)
- 1 tablespoon Oil

- 1 Egg

- 2 teaspoons Salt

- 3 tablespoons Sugar

- Jam to your taste

- Sugar and cinnamon to sprinkle

Mix yeast ingredients and let rest for 10 minutes.

Mix the yeast mix together with all the ingredients but the flour. Mix slowly the flour and work well. Let rest for 3 hours. Fry in hot and deep oil, measuring the batter with a large spoon.

Turn once to brown evenly. Drain over paper towels. When cool, fill with the jam and sprinkle with sugar an cinnamon.

96. Wine fritters

Yield: 4 Serving

Ingredient

- 4 Stick-type rolls
- 200 grams Flour (1 3/4 cups)
- 2 Eggs
- ¼ litre Milk
- 1 pinch Salt
- Fat for deep-frying
- ½ litre Wine OR cider
- Sugar to taste

Combine the flour, eggs, milk, and salt into a batter. Cut the rolls into 4 slices. Dip the slices into the batter, and then fry until golden brown.

Arrange fritters in a bowl, and pour hot, sweetened wine or cider over them. Give them time to soak up the wine before serving.

EDIBLE FLOWER FRITTTERS

97. Elderflower fritters served with elderflower mousse

Yield: 4 Serving

Ingredient

- Sunflower oil for deep frying
- 8 Heads elderflower; depending on size
- 180 grams Plain flour
- 1 tablespoon Caster sugar
- A pinch of salt
- Finely grated zest of 1 lemon
- 2 Eggs
- 60 milliliters Milk

- 60 milliliters Dry white wine
- 1 Wedges lemon and icing sugar

Sift the flour into a bowl with the sugar and salt. Add the lemon zest and eggs, and splash in about half the milk and half the wine. Begin whisking the liquids into the flour, gradually incorporating the rest of the milk and wine to make a smooth batter.

One by one, take the flowers by their stems and dunk into the batter. Lift out and let the excess batter run off, then slide into the oil.

After two minutes the underneath should be light golden brown. Turn the fritters and crisp for another minute. Drain on kitchen paper before serving.

98. Dandelion flower fritters

Yield: 10 Serving

Ingredient

- 1 cup Whole-Wheat Flour
- 2 tablespoons Olive Oil
- 2 teaspoons Baking Powder
- 1 cup Dandelion Flowers
- 1 pinch Salt
- 1 Egg
- Nonstick Vegetable-Oil Spray
- ½ cup Low-Fat Milk

This variation on pancakes uses the yellow puffs of the dandelion, a good source of Vitamin A.

In a bowl mix together flour, baking powder and salt. In a separate bowl, beat egg, and then mix with milk or water and olive oil.

Combine with dry mixture. Stir in yellow flowers carefully, taking care not to crush them.

Lightly spray a griddle or frying pan with vegetable oil.

Heat until thoroughly warmed. Pour batter onto griddle by spoonfuls and cook like pancakes.

99. Elderflower fritters

Yield: 1 Serving

Ingredient

- 8 Elderflower heads
- 110 grams Plain flour
- 2 tablespoons Sunflower oil
- 150 milliliters Lager or water
- 1 Egg white

- Oil for frying

- Icing sugar; sifted

- Lemon wedges

Sift the flour and salt together and mix to a batter with the oil and lager. Allow to stand in a cool place for 1 hour. Beat the egg white until it holds in stiff peaks. Fold in the egg just before using the batter.

Heat some oil in a deep pan or deep fryer. Dip the flower heads in the batter and then drop into the smoking hot oil and fry until golden brown.

Drain the fritters on kitchen paper. Pile on to a dish, sprinkle with the sifted icing sugar and serve with lemon wedges.

100. Rose petal fritters

Yield: 4 Serving

Ingredient

- 1 each bunch of rose petals
- confectioners' sugar
- sweet sauce

Toss the petals in and mix gently.

Drop into the hot oil and fry until golden.

To fry: Dip chunks of food into batter. Fry in 3-4 inches of fat at 375 degrees until golden brown.

Drain on paper toweling.

Sprinkle fruit fritters with confectioners' sugar or top with a sweet sauce.

CONCLUSION

Sweet or savoury, the humble fritter is deliciously versatile. Crisp and warm from the frying pan is our favourite best way to enjoy the dough-based dish, particularly as a part of a lazy weekend breakfast.

With a bit of care, it is easy to make homemade fritters that are a rich and decadent treat, suitable for breakfast, dinner, dessert, or just as a snack. There are a wide variety of fritter recipes in this book to try that are sure to please just about anyone.

Before you start making fritters, find the right batter that works for your kitchen and taste buds. Try this basic batter recipe that uses light tasting coconut oil for a refreshing flavor. Mix in your choice of different fillings, from sweet and fruity to meat and savory.

www.ingramcontent.com/pod-product-compliance
Lightning Source LLC
Chambersburg PA
CBHW050355120526
44590CB00015B/1697